DAWN
ANYWAY

DAWN ANYWAY

by Kate Lassman

DAWN ANYWAY

by Kate Lassman

Copyright © 2022
by Kate Lassman

Editors
Sandra Olivetti Martin and Noah Hale

New Bay Books
Fairhaven, Maryland
NewBayBooks@gmail.com

Design by Suzanne Shelden

Shelden Studios
Prince Frederick, Maryland
sheldenstudios@comcast.net

Cover Photo:
Cove Point Dawn, photo by Suzanne Shelden

A Note on Type: Cover and section heads are set in Sanvito.
The text font is based on Garamond Premier Pro.

Library of Congress
Cataloging-in-Publication Data
ISBN 978-1-7348866-9-6

Printed in the United States of America
First Edition

Contents

Preface	1

Summer

Dawn	4
Morning Glory	5
The Mantis	6
Dragonfly!	7
Seagull on Driftwood	8
Phoenix	9
Koi	10
The Shell	11
While the Light Lasts	12
Hearing a Perseid Meteor	13

Autumn

The Morning Glory Way	16
Lines to a Fox	17
Hope's Poem	18
On an Overcast Night	19
October Leaves	20
Stormclouds	21
November Sun	22
Street Light	23
After the First Frost	24
Chinese Take-out	25

Winter

Like the Moon	28
Advent	29
Icy	30
Insect Dreams	31
Missing Mary Oliver	32
January Daffodil	33
The Lake in Winter	34
New Orleans Ash Wednesday	35
Ballston Metro	36
Moonrise	37

Spring

Morning Broadcast	40
Courting	41
Ambivalence	42
Chimney Swifts	43
Seagull Song	44
Unbaffled	45
Day Trip to Solomon's Island	46
Stopped	47
Thunder at 3 am	48
Dawn Anyway	49

Acknowledgements	50
About the Author	51

Preface

These are poems of love, for the dawn and for the wider natural world. They explore the beauty of its landscapes and living creatures. For me, nature always retains such a marvelous sense of potentiality and hope, even in the darkest times.

Already the 21st century has tried us in new ways. Terrorist attacks, economic collapse, the effects of climate change, and a global pandemic have scarred our world. With this darkness surrounding us, it is all too easy to close ourselves off from others, from nature, and from ourselves. It is all too easy to despair.

Dawn Anyway wants to light a candle in this darkness, affirming the truth that there is still beauty, wisdom, meaning, and joy to be found in the world and in our lives. The poems in each section of the book celebrate nature as it has come to me in my daily life. I hope the poems will light a candle of hope for you as you read, as writing them has for me. No matter how dark a literal or metaphorical night may grow, dawn will follow anyway.

Kate Lassman

Summer

Dawn

"Dawn always tells us something, always."
—Adam Zagajewski

This is the most poetic time: a brisk and airy dawn,
before the gold horizon grows too florid,
before the noisy world wakes.
The sky glows with cobalt vibrancy
and the moon's full pearlescence.
Walk with me now—see, breathe,
listen in the deep, crisp silence,
and a still small voice may speak.

Morning Glory

The name of the morning glory
glows like a sunrise.
Its leaves flow over the trellis,
a cascade eager to bask
in early light.
Whether in rain or wind or fog or sun,
the celestial azure and white blooms
unfurl, rejoice in a new day
simply because it is
and they are here to savor it.

The Mantis

regards me with the same surprised and fragile curiosity
as I him, bright eyes from the insect world
questioning,
heart-shaped head tipped childlike.
A spring green twig for all the movement made,
he may think my fidgets impractical,
my blinking odd, my size gratuitous.
He then starts to sway, purposefully,
shifting small weight from my thumb to my wrist,
keeping folded arms, folded wings,
all poise.
Then abruptly, having seen
enough, the mantis departs in flight
with a noisy grace.

Dragonfly!

Just try to say the name without
a thrill of wonder. It can be no easier
than catching a living bit
of prism light in your extended palm.
Curious as cats, teasing as trout, they'll loop
a dizzying path around you, just close enough
to make a game of catching and of letting go
your breath. They spread a dusting of the joy
of color, of translucency, of flight,
then vanish in the instant
just before you realize you have seen
magic in the world.

Seagull on Driftwood
After the sculpture "Calling Gull" by Phyllis Noble

After long circling, a seagull lands
atop a knotted, tangled shape of wood
with lines and angles smoothed by water,
brown tones blended like an agate stone.
She folds her wings and lifts her head
and gives a joyful seagull-cry
saying simply, "This is mine;
I have found my place."

Phoenix

The tree that stood here must have been
magnificent. I envision linden branches
shielding grasses, housing birds,
hosting cicadas all the August long,
its sunlit leaves aglow
in emerald and jade.

The stump still left behind,
three paces in diameter,
dominates the yard,
despite the grass and clover
trying to cover it. I never found out why
the linden was cut down.

Three years pass; a sapling now grows,
flourishing, from the center
of the stump. Like a phoenix,
the little linden rises up
amid another August's fires, high already
as my upstretched hand can touch.

My love and I pour water on its roots.
Life, irrepressible, wonderfully perseveres.

Koi

Look into the pond
the way you'd look in a magic mirror
and you will see the speckled koi
as they ripple in serenity
through their own otherworldly realm.
Their fins fan them along,
darting or drifting;
together each fish
fits like tesserae,
each koi part of a slow
kaleidoscopic dance.
Stately, wise-eyed,
sagely floating in midpond:
living meditation, living calm.

The Shell

Almost luminous with living fire as it
turns in the light
as if carved out of tiger eye
swirled with ivory
the snail shell's power lies in
coils upon coils leading
inward ever tighter
like a fractal maze the eye
can get lost in,
wandering but immobile

While the Light Lasts

With the dusk come long distorted shadows;
sultry temperatures fade in their intensity.
The summer day—has it been wasted?—
is nearly at its close. In the grass
fireflies twinkle, since the stars
are not yet ready.
Under a willow, a flash—
once, twice, again. I cup my hand
beneath it, watch the insect
crawl across my palm.
Flash—a fleeting gift of light.
The firefly rises from my hand
and joins the others; their flickerings
surround me like a melody.
The sky dims, shadows stretch,
and colors deepen. I stay
cherishing the light
for as long as it lasts.

Hearing a Perseid Meteor

in sky clearer than a mirror
deep as absolute zero
skims a blue-lit fragment
close enough
to show an oblong shape
as it passes with a
soft slow alien whoosh
not quite like the wind

Autumn

The Morning Glory Way

I wake with my heart as overcast
as the sky, and do not even want
my first early walk of autumn.
I go nonetheless,
contemplating the asphalt
and scanning the trail's edge
for poison ivy.

Nearing home, the path curves eastward
and I stop stunned
by brilliant cobalt morning glories
climbing a neighbor's fence.
I'd not looked up to notice them before.

Given sun for their leaves, rain for their roots,
the pentagonal blooms face skyward,
joyful in their simple work
of being morning glories.
They need do no more.

I hope I will remember
when I go walking next
to go the morning glory way.

Lines to a Fox

I do not know what brought you to our street,
thin and lithe in dusky autumn fur,
pausing just as I glimpsed you,
head high despite not fitting in,
then trotting off with
eye-catching, slippery grace.
I do not believe in coincidence
and though you did not seem to find
whatever you came looking for,
in the sight of you here—risking, daring—
perhaps I did.

Hope's Poem

I need a poem.
I've been looking all day,
but found none
at the grocery store,
among the bills I paid,
or mixed with the laundry.
No poems today
in the painting above my desk
or in the music
loaded on my phone.
No poems today.
Then Hope, the regal brown tabby,
jumps on my lap and purrs.
I have a poem.

On An Overcast Night

So much for stargazing.
Clouds like cream in coffee
obscure the midnight sky,
pseudopods creeping along,
growing, melding, thickening, concealing,
disconcertingly solid
as if to block starlight forever.

All I can do is remind myself
that clouds are at their cores
illusionists;
they do not know the word
forever. With that,
with my telescope,
I resolve to return tomorrow.

October Leaves

An October wind
whorls through the grove of lindens
with a laughlike hiss;
showered in yellow leaves
I reach out to catch one.

Stormclouds

Plumbous clouds like mountains
rise above the rooftops,
dark against the pale sky
and mesmerizing
in their fluid advancement.

They are beautiful.
They are more beautiful
than a bright warm morning
monochrome and without depth.

A chill wind
is the most exhilarating
for it often is the storms
that do the cleansing
and the storms
that have the more dramatic beauty
and the storms
that make us stand alone
arrested, amazed, in awe.

November Sun

After a dim workday,
a dim drive home,
the car is parked at last.
As I walk, a rare light
beams through the murky sky
and a half-leaved treetop across the street
ignites into gold-orange glory,
reveling in the light despite
its bittersweet knowledge
of winter's coming.

Street Light

Tonight I watched a documentary
about the last Apollo astronauts.
Now through the window, maize light glows faintly
from a streetlamp. My life and these jots
will not make lasting marks on history,
but common ventures too are worth our thoughts.
The everyday gets brushed aside too soon—
a streetlamp lights the night as does the moon.

After the First Frost

The first frost has come and gone.
So have the birds,
and the squirrels
have taken to their burrows.
The trees stand stark and motionless,
leaves becoming dull brown dust underfoot.

A heavy sky remains,
but there will be no snow
to sparkle in the air
and anticipate the holidays.

On a day like this, how is it that
bright chrysanthemums like garnets
planted under the window
still find strength to bloom?

Chinese Take-Out

The sky has darkened,
yet he still won't be home for hours.
The cat is mewing by the door.

What is there to do
but try to quiet her with treats
and settle on the couch
with a movie he doesn't like
and Chinese take-out
for one

Winter

Like the Moon
(with apologies to Mark Nepo)

I've been told that poets
should aim, like the sun,
to shine with golden fire
from within.
Starfire warmth is wondrous,
but if it is required
then I am not a poet
and am cold.

I'm more like the moon.
I have craters, tides, and phases.
If you see me shining,
it's a gift of reflectivity
of a greater light than mine.
If that makes me pale, as I'm told,
that's okay.
I've always preferred silver over gold.

Advent

The night curls in smokily on itself
in deeply silenced disappointment.
Scanty artificial light leaks
in a puddle, jazz-joint dim, of rain and weariness.
The dusty day went on, went on
as ever many have, crawling like a cricket
with one hind leg, and now
all grows more still, blind and cold.
Nothing, nothing, patters the rain.
Nothing. Nowhere. Then
a spark of dawn gleams in the east
and this small place holds its breath.

Icy

The sun sets, leaving icy blue, then black
and who can say if it will rise again?
Branches of the silhouettes of trees
as unmoving as the wind is still—
they do not know what it is, like the water,
to break, break, break on rocky spires.

The snow falls, leaving icy gray on green
and who can say if we will grow old waiting
for it to melt again?
Until then may the wind stay still—
only the gull that has circled and cried
can know what it is to fall.

Insect Dreams

The seventeen-year cicada waits
hidden in an underground cell,
quietly feeding on tree root sap—
has it any assurance in its insect dreams
that a time will come to wake, to surface,
climb a tree and leave behind
its last hard brown instar shell,
and finally try its voice out, try its wings?

Missing Mary Oliver
After the painting "Great Egret" by Peggy Cook

If she were here at water's edge
Mary would have her notebook open,
composing lines about the great egret
surveying this pond.
It is winter; he has returned
to his dormant castle
of frigid water, bent cattails,
and grasses brown and brittle.
As he shakes his snowy feathers,
Mary would glean wisdom from the elegance
of his deliberate steps, see humor
glint in yellow eyes; then
laugh in wonder
at his sudden lift in flight.
Alone, I can only describe
the white-plumed monarch
and his reedy realm, only watch
as he fades flapping into January skies.

January Daffodil

January daffodil
encrusted in ice
like spun glass, like pearls.
So this is love.

The Lake in Winter

The lake is an uneasy sleeper.
It ripples vaguely
as the February wind
changes course;
subdued geese and mallards
meander its waters.

When it stills, the surface
is a tarnished silver
that absorbs more winter light
than it reflects.
It is a glass that I see through darkly,
wishing now for wakefulness,
wishing now for Spring.

New Orleans Ash Wednesday

One silent hour after
the midnight whistle blew;
a gilded, feathered mask in the street
the smell of gumbo fading
the stars dimmer.

Ballston Metro

I wait on the train platform
among bundled commuters
fluttering their wings in eagerness
beneath the concrete honeycomb that
arcs over our heads, awaiting Spring
to leave this droning hive
in search of nectar.

Moonrise
After the painting "Moonrise Over Back Creek, Solomon's" by Julie Allinson

A chill night
of not-quite-spring
silent and bleak-black
no stars, no light
raw wind and haze—
Is this where you are?

I have been there.
Turn around. The river
is still rippling.
Turn around. See the rise
of blue mist over the water—
See the moon.

Spring

Morning Broadcast

The birds high up
on the transmission tower
chatter loudly as cerulean
light warms to copper, then to gold,
together broadcasting
the most important news of the day:
It is dawn.

Courting

Two
gray
squirrels
Swishscuffle
And skitter
Up and
around,
down and
about the
convoluted
Branches of the
tall and
patient
linden tree

Ambivalence

My cat
crouches in front of the
sliding glass door,
transfixed,
watching the floodrains
waterfall off the roof,
from off the trees,
from everywhere.
She paws the door, pulls back,
paws it again;
her full moon eyes
glow.

Chimney Swifts

"As kingfishers catch fire, dragonflies draw flame"
—Gerard Manley Hopkins

Out earning its name
just after dawn the swift
skims over the pond.
Then two of them are,
dipping and darting,
rippling the surface,
kiting away, returning,
thinking like
the kingfisher to catch the fire
from the sun reflected
in the shining water.

Seagull Song

It perches near-forgotten on
the curio cabinet shelf,
the porcelain seagull music box,
a birthday gift some years ago.
I haven't touched it, heard it play
in many a mundane month.

Tonight I find my thoughts wound down
and flightless, crumbling into sand.
I'm moved to hold the music box,
hear it sing "By the Beautiful Sea."
Perhaps the song will set the seagull free
in me.

Unbaffled

A black squirrel navigates
the tightrope branch,
tail as a balance pole,
reaches the dangling rope,
slithers down headfirst
and stretches out a paw into
the newly filled
birdfeeder.

Day Trip to Solomon's Island
After the painting "Waiting at Solomon's Island"
by Carol Wade

I have never been sailing.
I haven't swum in years.
Cautions in my father's voice
fill the back of my mind.

Yet here we are: a day off,
a clear May morning,
a picturesque island coast,
a rustic wooden dock
spanning limpid, languid water,
a simple boat, shrill seagull voices,
your smile as you extend your hand.

I smile back and take it. "Yes, let's go."

Stopped

Stopped in traffic, I'm captive
as one by one, a family
of Canada geese, two parents
and five goslings, cross the city road.
They stroll between cars, heedless
of the turn of traffic lights,
the threat of glass and steel,
and most of all, post-work humans.
I wait for them, unsure
whether to admire their courage
or astonish at their chutzpah.

Thunder at 3AM

It splits the warm and velvet night
like the Red Sea, sends the cat
running, in a breach of feline dignity,
to hurdle onto the bed, escaping
toward the promise of a reassuring arm.

Dawn Anyway

It's happened now so many times
it no longer stuns:
a storm, a blaze, a violent attack,
an outbreak, or a drought.
People call for more security or aid,
politicians send their thoughts and prayers,
then the moment passes,
but it leaves shattering behind,
slow-healing wounds, and tears.

The next day, a new sun paints the clouds
in salmon, orchid, cream, and fire
between turquoise and mist.
In the stillness as the sparrows sing,
we wake in spite of everything;
after storm-filled starless endless nights
dawn comes anyway.

Acknowledgements

Thanks to the following periodicals in which earlier versions of some of the poems in this collection first appeared:

The Avocet and *The Weekly Avocet*:
"Lines to a Fox"; "The Shell"; "Stormclouds"; "The Mantis"; "Koi"; "The Lake in Winter"; "Insect Dreams"; "On an Overcast Night"; "The Morning Glory Way"; "Seagull on Driftwood"; "Moonrise"; "Missing Mary Oliver"; and "Chimney Swifts" (republication)

Connections:
"Morning Glory"; "Hearing a Perseid Meteor" "October Leaves"; "Hope's Poem"

Nibble:
"Thunder at 3AM"

The Northern Virginia Review:
"Chimney Swifts"; "Morning Broadcast"; "New Orleans Ash Wednesday"

Time of Singing:
"Advent"; "After the First Frost"

"Hope's Poem" and "Seagull Song" were included in the volume *Pax: An Anthology of Southern Maryland Poetry*, published by Wineberry Press, 2019.

Thanks to the calvART Gallery in Prince Frederick, Maryland for including "The Mantis" and "Koi" in the *Visions and Verses* exhibit April 11–May 6, 2018, and "Seagull on Driftwood" April 11–May 5, 2019.

Thanks to the Calvert Library in Prince Frederick, Maryland for including "Day Trip to Solomon's Island" in the *Water/Ways Traveling Smithsonian Institution Exhibition* January 25–March 6, 2020

I also wish to thank my husband David Lassman, my sister Shary Moose Kranch, my mother Irene Moose, my friends Sue Wright and Christy Smith, and the members of the Southern Maryland Poetry Circle for all their support, beta reading, and workshop advice. Thanks also to editors Sandra Olivetti Martin and Noah Hale for making this book possible.

The Author on Her Life

I grew up the daughter of a geophysicist and a children's librarian, Fred and Irene Moose, and with a sister, Shary, who would become an archaeologist. The suburb of Denver, Colorado, where we lived was part of Englewood at the time, but later, in 2001, the residents would vote to incorporate it as the separate town of Centennial.

My interest in both writing and nature came very early. My mother taught my sister and me about the backyard birds and about the vegetables and flowers we grew in the garden. In summer my father would take us all on day trips up into the mountains for picnics and long lovely walks. As a child I was always writing little stories; then in high school at age 16, I fell in love with poetry. I think it was that year when I first read the poem "Pied Beauty" by Gerard Manley Hopkins.

I began study at Grove City College as a biology major, with the idea of becoming an entomologist. I eagerly enrolled in the department's entomology course the first time it was ever offered. Besides learning many wonderful things about insects in that class, I also learned that my interest in them is a writer's interest rather than a scientist's. I graduated from Grove City with a double major, with English as the primary one.

Afterward I worked at a bookstore and earned an MFA in poetry from George Mason University. My poems began being published in magazines. I also met my husband, David Lassman, who was also working at the bookstore and pursuing a degree (in his case, in history) at George Mason. We married after we both finished our degrees.

I taught writing and literature at Northern Virginia Community College, until David got his dream job as a park ranger and we moved to Maryland. I then started teaching at the College of Southern Maryland. I also joined the Maryland Writers' Association and the Southern Maryland Poetry Circle. In 2019, I contributed two poems when the poetry circle released an anthology entitled Pax: An Anthology of Southern Maryland Poetry, published by The Wineberry Press.

Together David and I love travelling, visiting antique malls and used book stores, and playing Scrabble. We also adopted rescue cats Hope, Joy, Grace, and Zany, thereby happily becoming the neighborhood's crazy cat people.

www.ingramcontent.com/pod-product-compliance
Lightning Source LLC
Chambersburg PA
CBHW020303030426
42336CB00010B/890